The editors would like to thank
BARBARA KIEFER, Ph.D.,
Charlotte S. Huck Professor of Children's Literature,
The Ohio State University, and
PAUL L. SIESWERDA, Aquarium Curator (retired),
New York Aquarium,·
for their assistance in the preparation of this book.

Visit us on the Web!
Seussville.com
randomhousekids.com

Educators and librarians, for a variety of teaching tools, visit us at
RHTeachersLibrarians.com

Library of Congress Cataloging-in-Publication Data
Worth, Bonnie.
Hark! a shark! : all about sharks / by Bonnie Worth ;
illustrated by Aristides Ruiz and Joe Mathieu. — 1st ed.
   p. cm. — (The Cat in the Hat's learning library)
Includes bibliographical references.
ISBN 978-0-375-87073-6 (trade) — ISBN 978-0-375-97073-3 (lib. bdg.)
1. Sharks—Juvenile literature. I. Ruiz, Aristides, ill. II. Mathieu, Joseph, ill. III. Title.
QL638.9.W68 2013
597.3—dc23
2011048247

MANUFACTURED IN CHINA   31

Hark! A Shark!

by Bonnie Worth

illustrated by Aristides Ruiz and Joe Mathieu

The Cat in the Hat's Learning Library®

Random House 🏠 New York

I'm the Cat in the Hat,
and for more than a lark,
would you care to go to
a brand-new kind of park?

In a super shark tank
that is like a small sea,
we will visit with sharks.
Do you dare come with me?

Sharks seem very scary
to us, it is true.
But most sharks are really
no danger to you.

People fear sharks,
and that's mostly because
of films that star sharks
with big, snapping jaws.

But give sharks a chance
and I think you will find
they will dazzle your eyes
and broaden your mind.

See this wonderful boat
bobbing here on the water?
It's my Super-Stupendous
Shipshape Shark Spotter.

For tracking down sharks
it's the best, don't you know?
So hop on aboard and
shark spotting we'll go!

Over four hundred species
swim the seas today.
Let's visit with some of them.
Anchors aweigh!

Sharks have been around
long before the dinosaur.
About four hundred million
years—maybe more!

MAN

MEGALODON
PREHISTORIC SHARK

Fossils of shark teeth
simply abound.
More than two hundred species
to date have been found.

We never find bones
because sharks don't have those.
Sharks are made up of car-ti-lage,
just like your nose!

Cartilage helps sharks
to turn and to bend
and to move through the water
much faster, my friend.

Like a brave knight's
thick suit of mail,
a shark's skin protects it
almost without fail.

Stroke the skin head to tail.
It is smooth, you will see.
Stroke the skin tail to head.
It's as rough as can be.

That's because it has den-ti-cles—
hard, toothy stuff
that lies flat for swimming
but makes the skin tough.

A whale's skin gets dirty
and gunky, you see.
But a shark's skin stays clean
and is nearly gunk-free.

It's tough and it's rough
and it's sleek and it's clean.
Shark skin's unlike anything
you've ever seen!

These fake sharkskin suits
help swimmers to win.

Human skin grafts
are grown from sharkskin.

And gunk falls right off of
the Shark Spotter's side
because of a paint that is
rough like shark hide.

Looking for sharks' teeth?
There are plenty—know why?
Most sharks have a nearly
unending supply.

From a jaw made of bone
your human teeth grow.
Shark teeth grow from gums
in row after row.

When a tooth becomes loose
or else gets a bad crack,
it will soon be replaced
by a tooth in the back.

What type of food will
your average shark choose?
Most sharks hunt for meat
when they go out to cruise.

Great whites' teeth are sharp
for tearing and munching.
Horn sharks' teeth are flat
for crushing and crunching.

HORN SHARK

17

GREAT WHITE

WHALE SHARK

This shark you see here
might fill you with awe,
but the tiniest teeth
fill its giant maw.

It's the largest shark
that you'll ever meet.
We measured it and
it is forty-four feet!

What is our giant friend's
favorite dish?
Plants and animals called plankton
and wee, tiny fish.

These gill rakers here
act just like a sieve.
They sift out the food
the whale shark needs to live.

When a shark swims along,
its mouth opens wide.
Water that comes in
goes out gills on the side.

TAIL

Its tail beats the water
and swings side to side.
See how smoothly
this leopard shark
here seems to glide?

PECTORAL FIN

Pectoral fins lift—
I have been thinking—
like two airplane wings,
to keep sharks from sinking.

Dorsal fins on the top
stand up and are ready
to keep sharks upright,
swimming even and steady.

DORSAL FIN

With its wide pectorals,
the angel shark lies flat
and as still as a rug—
will you just look at that?

It's so still that you might
think that it is just napping.
Then suddenly, look!
Its strong jaws are snapping.

The shark comes equipped
with a keen inner ear
that senses whenever
its prey might be near.

INNER EAR

NARES

And the nostril-like holes
that sit under its snout
sniff out any prey
that is lurking about.

The name that we give
these two holes is *nares*.
It's helpful to know that
the word rhymes with *fairies*.

Nurse sharks have whiskers,
and what are they for?
These whiskers—called barbels—
sweep the seafloor.

These whiskery gizmos
do not go to waste.
The shark uses them
to feel and to taste.

BARBELS

LATERAL LINE

There's a line of pores
along a shark's sides.
The pores are like sensors
set into sharks' hides.
They pick up vibrations
from prey all around,
cluing sharks as to where
their prey can be found.

Most sharks, as a rule,
have quite keen eyesight.
Their eyes can see well
in both dim and bright light.

The puffadder shyshark's
long tail whips around
and helps hide it from predators,
shark experts have found.

The hammerhead shark's range of sight overlaps, giving it much better vision, perhaps.

But who needs sharp eyes way down deep in the murk, where this rare goblin shark's nose does all of the work?

Some sharks are hatched
out of eggs in a case
that is hidden by Mom
in a very safe place.

BABY

EGG

YOLK
SAC

Some shark eggs hatch
inside Mom and then thrive
on egg yolk till they're
big enough to survive.

Lemon sharks, like us,
as I have just read,
grow in their moms' bodies,
where they're safe and fed.

This pup is born live,
rests a bit, and then, hark!
Off it goes on its own.
That's the life of a shark!

Thing Two has come up
with this most clever verse.
An empty egg case is
called a mermaid's purse!

Tagging is how
we have learned very much
about many sharks' habits
and movements and such.

Lemon sharks get tagged
and do not seem to mind.

Other sharks mind it plenty,
I think you will find.

Tags offer data,

like this bit, for instance:

a blue shark can swim

a very long distance.

NEW YORK

134Z5E

BRAZIL

In sixteen months' time,

from New York it will

swim four thousand miles

to far-off Brazil.

The Things are now holding
a Shark Spotter contest
to reward each shark here
for what it does the best.

BIGGEST

The whale shark is biggest.
We've said this before.

The smallest?
Dwarf lantern shark—
about eight inches, no more.

SMALLEST

The fastest is mako.
It is a speed whiz.

The wobbegong might be
the slowest there is.

What sort of shark
is this that I spot?
It looks like a thresher shark
here, does it not?

It has a long tail.
See how that tail swishes
to round up its dinner,
a mouthful of fishes?

LONGEST TAIL

LONGEST TAIL

1st PLACE

The tiger shark isn't fussy.
It'll eat anything.
A clock or a stool
or a rusty bedspring.

LEAST FUSSY EATER

The cookie-cutter shark
with its big teeth rips
neat, perfect circles,
sucked free with its lips.

NEATEST BITE

The spiny dogfish—
just call him granddad—

lives as long as some humans.
That's some life he's had!

LONGEST LIFE

The megamouth attacks prey.
It glows in the dark.
Light works as a lure
for this deepwater shark.

BRIGHTEST SMILE

BEST TEAM-WORK

These whitetip reef sharks
sometimes swim in packs
and hunt as a team for
their favorite snacks.

The spinner shark here confuses its prey by spinning its body in a dizzying way.

COOLEST MOVE

MOST FEARED!

The great white looks deadly upon close inspection but may be in danger without our protection.

Our visit is over.
But hold on! Not quite!
Let's spend some more time
with the deadly great white.

The great white is simply
a hunting machine.
Watch it at work
and you'll see what I mean.

Dark on its top side
and lighter below,
it can sneak up no matter
the angle, you know.

Its jaws jut out far
(the better to grip).
Its teeth are made so
as to bite and to rip.

Its big head shakes hard
to loosen and snatch.
Its eyes roll far back,
avoiding a scratch.

If you swim where it's safe,
sharks will leave you be.
You will stay as safe
as on land, you will see.

Around this hard fact
I will not haw or hem:
sharks should fear us
more than we do them.

Sharks are in danger.
This I will repeat.
People hunt them down
for sport and for meat,
for oil and for
their remarkable skins,
and let's not forget
for their dorsal fins.

SHARK LIVER
OIL SOAP

ANTI-AGING
CREAM

People are not the
shark's natural prey.
But too many people
think it's that way.

They want to get sharks
before sharks get us.
Let's speak for the sharks
and stir up a fuss.

Do your bit to help.
Here's what you might say
to shark fin soup supper—
just say *yuck, no way!*
Do not go shark fishing
just for a lark.
Let's let the sharks be.

Yes! Let's save the shark!

GLOSSARY

Abound: To be in great numbers.

Fossil: The remains of an animal or plant from the distant past.

Graft: A surgical process to replace damaged skin with healthy skin, either taken from another part of the body or made in a laboratory.

Lure: Something that brings prey closer so it can be eaten, such as a worm tied to a fishing line.

Maw: The throat and jaws of a hungry animal.

Sensor: Something that detects or measures a signal.

Sieve: A device that separates wanted from unwanted material, using tiny holes that let only smaller particles and liquids get through.

Species: A group of living things that can get together and produce offspring.

Vibration: The rapid back-and-forth motion of an object or substance.

FOR FURTHER READING

Face to Face with Sharks by David Doubilet and Jennifer Hayes (National Geographic Children's Books, *Face to Face with Animals*). Up-close underwater photographs illustrate this book in an award-winning series. For ages 6–9.

Hungry, Hungry Sharks! by Joanna Cole, illustrated by Patricia Wynne (Random House, *Step into Reading,* Step 3). An easy-to-read introduction to sharks. For ages 5–8.

Sharkabet: A Sea of Sharks from A to Z by Ray Troll (WestWinds Press/American Museum of Natural History). A fun look at twenty-six different sharks—and the alphabet! For ages 6 and up.

Sharks by Seymour Simon (HarperCollins, *Smithsonian*). An introduction to sharks by a highly acclaimed children's science writer. Illustrated with photographs. For ages 6–10.

Swimming with Hammerhead Sharks by Kenneth Mallory (Sandpiper, *Scientists in the Field*). A look at hammerheads with one of the world's leading experts. Illustrated with photographs. For ages 10–12.

INDEX

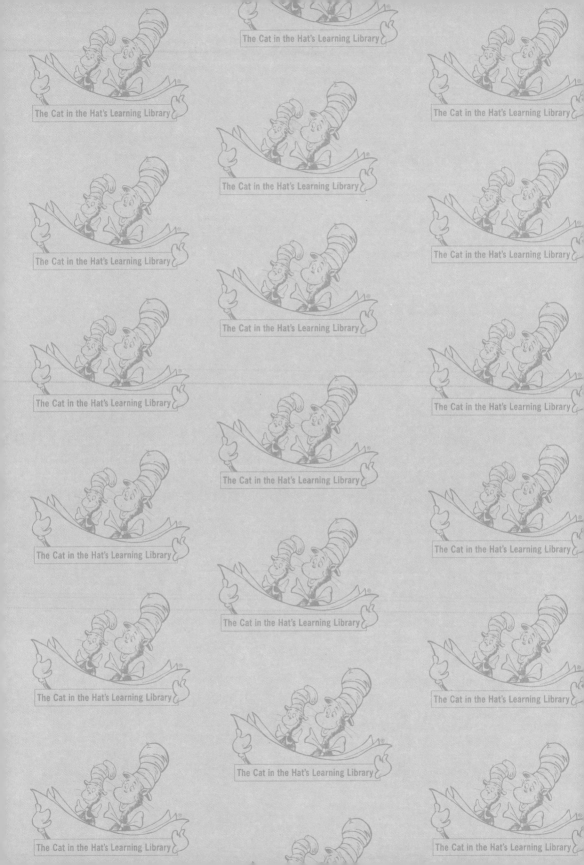